THE SIMPLE GUIDE TO
CUSTOMS AND ETIQUETTE
IN
ISRAEL

ABOUT THE AUTHOR

DAVID STARR-GLASS is a college administrator and a senior lecturer in management studies at several American colleges in Jerusalem. Born in Scotland in 1948, he converted to Judaism in 1974. He worked as an accountant in California before emigrating with his family to Israel in 1983. Keenly interested in religious affairs, he is also the author of *Gathered Stones* (Feldheim: 1994) and the *Simple Guide to Judaism* (Global Books: 1996)

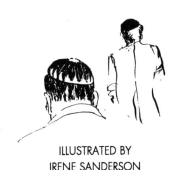

ILLUSTRATED BY
IRENE SANDERSON

THE SIMPLE GUIDE TO CUSTOMS AND ETIQUETTE IN

ISRAEL

DAVID STARR-GLASS

GLOBAL BOOKS LTD

Simple Guides • Series 1
CUSTOMS & ETIQUETTE

The Simple Guide to
CUSTOMS & ETIQUETTE IN ISRAEL
by David Starr-Glass

First published in 1996 by
GLOBAL BOOKS LTD
P.O. Box 219, Folkestone, Kent, England CT20 3LZ

© Global Books Ltd 1996

ISBN 1–86034–055–5

British Library Cataloguing in Publication Data
A CIP catalogue entry for this book
is available from the British Library

Distributed in the USA & Canada by:
The Talman Co. Inc
131 Spring Street
New York, NY 10012
USA

Set in Futura 11 on 12 pt by Bookman, Slough
Printed in Great Britain by
The Cromwell Press Ltd., Broughton Gifford, Wiltshire

Contents

Preface

Jerusalem's contrasting skyline: Russian monastery
and the Dome of the Rock

In the days of the Talmud – some eighteen hundred years
ago – Rabbi Ashi journeyed to Machuza. They said to
him: 'Master, make the Great Kiddush for us.' He did not
know what they meant by the Great Kiddush, but he
reasoned that it must contain the blessing: 'He who made
the fruit of the vine', and so that is how he started out.
Others say that he said the blessing: 'He who made the
fruit of the vine', and then paused. He saw an old man
start to drink his wine and realized that he need say no
more. Of Rabbi Ashi it was said, 'The wise man has eyes
in his head', (Ecclesiastes 2:14).

Babylonian Talmud, Pesachim 106

Customs are embedded in the culture matrix
of a people; etiquette is a more refined
external veneer. Both require time to develop
and to bubble up to the surface. Israel has been
a state for less than fifty years. Has it had time
to develop distinct customs and etiquette?

You will find that Israel is still digesting the
differences of the peoples who have come
from every country that you have ever heard of
– and a few more besides. You, too, would do
best to follow Robert Ashi's example: become

an observer of those around you. Do not jump to conclusions. Israel *is* different than your home country – and from what you expect it to be. Keep your eyes and ears open. Keep your mind open as well.

D.S-G

1

Changing Culture – Changing Custom

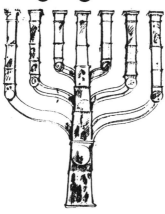

The Menorah – symbol of the State of Israel and
Jewish faith

B'ruchim ha'bayim l'Eretz Yisrael! Blessings to you who
have come (or are coming) to Israel!

You are visiting a country with a remarkable
history and a vibrant potential. For the
most part the Israelis you meet will greet you
cordially and will be appreciative of your
presence in their country. As a guest you will
be afforded genuine hospitality and you will not
be expected to understand the ways of your
hosts; even Israelis find themselves difficult to
understand at times!

You will find that Israeli public behaviour is
very relaxed, casual, flexible with indivi-
dual eccentricity hardly noticed. Often what
you witness might seem brash, impetuous or
even rude. In private you will find Israelis less
volatile and capable of developing warm,

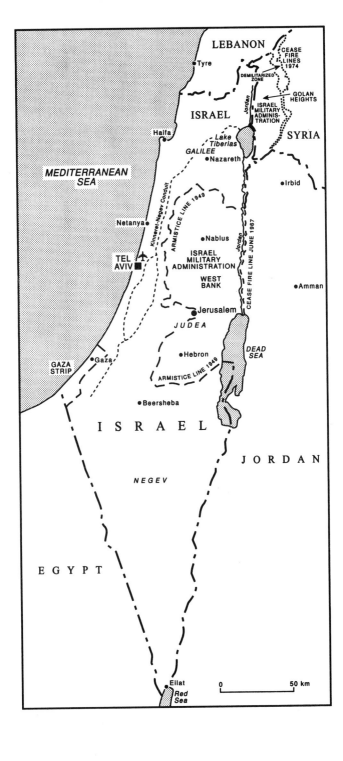

sincere relationships. Always keep in mind that Israel is a land of contrast, paradox and unpredictability.

This guide is meant to give you some appreciation of the customs which you will observe on your visit. It cannot be (nor is it intended to be) an in-depth exploration of the Israeli psyche, and yet you do have to understand something of the development of that psyche in order to appreciate the national identity of this country.

A BRIEF HISTORICAL OVERVIEW

Some 4,000 years ago the Patriarchs (Avraham, Itzchak and Ya'akov) walked over the hills of Israel. In Jewish tradition, this land was promised to them. It was the children of Ya'akov (who was later called Yisrael) who eventually returned from slavery in Egypt to claim their divine inheritance; this is the land of Yisrael's children.

By about 1200 BCE ('Before the Christian Era') the country had been secured and

'. . .where Abraham walked'

MAP OF ISRAEL
Note: The Gaza Strip, and most of the major Arab population centres in Judea and the West Bank, are controlled by the Palestinian Authority.

was administered by a system of Judges. By about 1000 BCE this system had given way to a Jewish monarchy centred on Jerusalem. A schism soon developed with two states – Israel and Judah – emerging. Both of these entities, as well as the Temple in Jerusalem, were destroyed by Nebuchadnezzar in 587 BCE. In the years which followed there were mass deportations to Babylon.

Jews returned from exile to establish a Second Temple. However, there was no lasting stability in the area. The cultural influence of the Greeks was strong and antagonistic to traditional Jewish teaching. The revolt of the Maccabees (165 BCE) while popularly celebrated – every year, at Chanukka – brought little lasting change.

Israel then fell under the domination of the Romans who eventually destroyed the Second Temple (70 CE – 'Christian Era') and brutally suppressed the Jewish uprising. The country – which the Romans called Palestine – was laid to waste and her Jewish population dispersed. This was the beginning of a 2,000-year exile or diaspora of the Jewish people from their homeland.

With no significant Jewish population left, Israel was governed by a succession of Byzantine and Arab dynasties until 1187 CE when, following early Christian victories during the Crusades, Jerusalem – and most of Israel – was captured by Saladin. The land was to remain firmly under Moslem control (Mamluke and Ottoman Turks) until 1917, when the Turkish governor surrendered to British forces. During the last 50 years of Turkish rule there had been repeated waves of Jewish immigration from Europe.

The British Mandate (1923–48) tried to administer a territory with growing, and fractious, Arab and Jewish communities. Despite a plan to partition the country (forming separate Jewish and Arab states), escalating violence, invasion of neighbouring Arab states, and finally a British withdrawal, threatened to annihilate the unborn Jewish state. The State of Israel was actually proclaimed on 14 May 1948 and straight away she found herself engaged in a war for independence.

Kibbutz

THE ORIGINAL ISRAELI SELF-IMAGE (1948–73)

The State of Israel was founded in 1948, as a direct result of the Holocaust, in which six million European Jews were murdered and reduced to ash. It would be difficult to overestimate the effect of this atrocity on the Israeli psyche. In the newly-formed State many Israelis saw a vehicle for reclaiming the dignity and freedom which had been inhumanly ripped away from them in Europe. Many senior Israelis are survivors of the death camps.

During the first twenty years of its existence the State was officially seen as a cultural melting pot:-

● Older cultural remnants, whether from Europe or from the Arabic-speaking world, were actively disapproved of by an overclass which was Zionistic, socialist and secular.

- Hebrew was the language of integration.
- Service in the Israeli Defence Forces was the main instrument of socialization.
- Attempts were made to invent a distinctive Israeli tradition in such areas as folk-dance, music, pageantry, cuisine etc.

During this period good manners were suspect and bourgeois; frankness and a hard-headed approach to all things was required; hard work was meritorious. The Israeli was to be proud, free, determined, idealistic, impetuous and supremely self-confident. This prickly image was mirrored in an economy which was idiosyncratic, isolated and predominantly controlled by the State. The collective farm (*kibbutz*) was considered to symbolize the correct values of society and economy. This prickly image still exists in many areas of government and has been widely exported as a stereotype.

THE CHANGED ISRAELI SELF-IMAGE (1973–93)

Following their precarious victory in the Yom Kippur War (1973), Israelis were forced to

The prickly pear cactus (*sabra*)

reexamine their original image of self. Many factors forced this quite dramatic re-appraisal, and led to a more mature, realistic image of what this dynamic country is all about:

- Disillusionment with government and politics in general.

- Regained ethnic pride among those from North African countries (the *S'fardim* – literally the descendants of the 'Spanish' Jews who were expelled from there in 1492) and those coming from the Yemen (the 'Oriental Jews').

- High inflation and a rolling devaluation of the Israeli currency.

- Ongoing belligerence with Arab neighbours.

- Growing scepticism of the army's intelligence/prowess.

During this period bad manners were increasingly seen as outbursts of frustration; persistence was seen as different from stubbornness; people were expected to work smarter, not necessarily harder. The Israeli was increasingly seen as having become a good regional, as well as world, citizen. Self-confidence drooped and was replaced by self-criticism.

Today, less than 4% of Israelis live on *kibbutzim*. Some 85% of the population lives in urban communities. The market-place has pushed aside State control of the economy (although remember that 25% of the gross national product is still derived from enterprises run by the State or labour unions/cooperatives).

THE PEACE PROCESS (1994 AND ONWARDS)

A new, but very uncertain, era began in Israel's history when it entered into peace agreements with the Palestine Authority and Jordan. The process was persistently and courageously pushed forward by Prime Minister – and former Chief of Staff – Itzchak Rabin. It is proving to be a contentious and deeply divisive process. The assassination of Mr Rabin (November, 1995) threw the country into a period of profound introspection and uncertainty. It is obvious that the next few years are going to be crucial in reshaping Israel's future and her image of self but it is unclear what that new image will look like.

Many people – world Jewry, friends of Israel and even Israelis themselves – are bewildered by this new, uncharted era. For many, the old pioneer myth was easier to identify with and to understand.

Native-born Israelis call themselves *sabras* – the fruit of the prickly pear cactus. The sabra is simply a spiny fruit with a very off-putting outside and deliciously sweet inside. Is this an accurate image of the average Israeli, or simply a comforting myth? You will have the opportunity to investigate for yourself. This guide will help you to avoid some of the more obvious spines and may even let you enjoy the inner fruit.

ISRAEL AND THE REST OF THE WORLD

Israelis love to travel, even though this is expensive for them. Europe, and especially the western end of the Mediterranean is the favourite holiday haunt. Many young people trek out to the Far East (India, Nepal, Thailand etc) after completing army service.

In spite of this, and their amazing ethnic diversity (they have come as immigrants from more than eighty different countries), Israelis are often very provincial in their dealings with foreigners.

In Hebrew, when you leave Israel you go 'out of the Land' (*chutz l'aretz* – usually contracted to *ch'l*); Israel is the centre of the world for most Israelis. There are sizeable communities of expatriate Israelis in America, Europe and Asia. They will often leave one another with the expression: *L'hitra'ot ba'aretz* – see you back in Israel. It is more often than not simply a pleasantry.

Remember that Israelis are very sensitive of their image as portrayed in the international media. They universally – and with some justification – regard it as negative, slanted and biased against them. This negativity has been compounded by a siege mentality on the part of Israelis at many times in Israeli's history.

Remember that an Israeli will probably assume that it is impossible for a person from outside – from *chutz l'aretz* – to understand him. Equally, keep in mind that any attempt you make to bridge the gap will be much appreciated.

Remember also, that Israel is a place of rich ethnic diversity. Like you, most of the people around you have come from different lands with different languages, customs and attitudes. Be sensitive to that and look out for expressions of this heterogeneity in the people you deal with. 'Unity in Diversity' is the official line and, for all its glibness, it does reflect the widely-held desire for a more unified Israeli society.

POPULATION

The population of Israel is a little under six million. Of these about 14% are Moslems (Arabs, predominantly Sunnis), 3% are Christians (90% of whom are Arabs) and smaller localized populations of Druze and Circassians (about 2%). This means that about 81% of Israelis are Jews.

Of the present Jewish population about 61% were born in Israel (*sabras*). Of the other 39% a third immigrated from Asian and African countries and two-thirds from Europe and the Americas. Since 1948 almost two-and-a-half million people have immigrated to Israel, more than half of them from Europe. Particularly noticeable are the new immigrants from Ethiopia.

While Israeli citizenship is awarded without reference to ethnic or religious origin, any Jew can petition under the Law of Return for citizenship. A little more than a third of world Jewry currently live in Israel.

Arab market

2

Food & Drink

Family celebrating *seder* at Passover
[A meal at which the story of the Passover is related,
and *matza* – bitter herbs – are eaten.]

Israel has not really developed a distinctive cuisine. You will find eating a cosmopolitan experience, with a great variety of food choices imported from Europe and North Africa. In general, the quality and preparation of food in public eating places is fairly basic and lacks ingenuity or invention.

The average Israeli enjoys the experience of eating more than the quality of the cooking; elaborate cuisine is still considered as little suspect. Notwithstanding that Puritanical prejudice, the quality of food offered in major hotels is good and has improved considerably in recent years.

Snack-taking is common. On most city streets you can find snack bars providing the North African *falafel* (fried chickpea batter, served with salads in pita bread) and *sh'warma* (slices of freshly roasted lamb served in a large pita roll), French-style baguette (open sandwiches with meat and/or salad) or Italian-style pizza. These are best eaten in the place where bought; eating them in the street is messy although not actually considered impolite.

When buying prepared food always check for cleanliness and freshness. Avoid anything which is not prepared directly in front of you. Buy from larger places where the turnover is high. If in doubt look for a better place: it is not worth an upset stomach.

You can eat all forms of ices, ice-cream and frozen yoghurt in the street without worrying about decorum. Israelis are especially fond of walking about munching fresh roasted sunflower seeds (*garanim*), pumpkin seeds, peanuts and pistachios. You can buy them by weight (in 100 grams increments) from most sweet shops.

Cooked food tends to be light, and lots of fresh fruits and vegetables are served. The tomato, egg-plant/aubergine (*chatzelim*) and bell-peppers turn up in various guises. The tomato in particular is considered indispensable in the standard Israeli cuisine; the monthly index of inflation has, on occasion, been pushed up by the exceedingly high prices paid for out-of-season tomatoes. Lettuce is not generally used in salads.

Chicken and turkey are inexpensive and widely eaten. Fish is excellent, while beef is expensive and less favoured. Standard Western fare is served in most hotels and tourist restaurants. In the larger cities ethnic restaurants (Chinese, French, Italian, Thai etc) are well represented but tend to be expensive.

Pavement cafes in Tel Aviv

The main meal of the day is still served early in the afternoon, with a light breakfast and supper. This is changing and it is increasingly common for the main meal to be in the evening. Hotels tend to serve substantial breakfasts. Formal meals are usually scheduled for the evening.

Table etiquette is very relaxed. Use your knife and/or fork in any way which is natural for you. After having cut the food it is common to lay the knife down and eat with the fork in the right hand (American style).

Eating customs are informal and reflect Israeli cultural diversity. If you have been invited for a meal at an Israeli home and have finished eating, you will inevitably be offered more food, which you will be expected to eat. If you do not wish to eat any more leave a small portion on your plate and move it away from you.

When you sit down with others to eat (or if you pass by someone who is eating) it is polite to wish them the Hebrew equivalent of the French *bon appetit* – *b'tai'avon* (literally: 'to your appetite') or *l'vri'ut* ('to your health').

In religious circles a formal meal will often begin with the ritual washing of hands and blessing made over bread dipped in salt. Ask your host if you are unsure what is happening.

Although most Israelis are not religiously observant, many are sensitive to *kashrut*, that is the eating of religiously permissible foods. The rules are complex and beyond the scope of this book – besides, you would not be expected to know them. Do remember that meat and milk products should not be eaten at the same meal. ('Meat' means all forms of red meat and poultry, but not fish.) Coffee will be served black if the meal consisted of meat. A non-dairy creamer is usually available: do not ask for milk.

Increasingly, restaurants and hotels are including a service charge (tip) in the cost of the meal. Look for this on the bill; do not confuse it with the consumer tax (VAT) which also appears. If a tip has not been included you are not obliged to leave one unless you think the service was exceptionally good. The normal tip is about 10% of the bill.

Unfortunately, service is still undervalued in most Israeli establishments. The good news is that it has improved dramatically over the last ten years. You can help this process

New-style shopping

along by insisting on courtesy and service, especially in establishments which cater to tourists. Of course, you may understandably opt for a quieter life.

Israelis do not drink a great deal of alcohol. You will rarely be offered it when you visit. Alcohol is considered appropriate only in very convivial male company, or at a celebration of some kind. On such occasions toasts are common. The traditional toast is, of course, *l'chaim!* (to life).

While there are many new pubs in Israel you might find the price, quality of beer and service unimpressive. Domestically produced beers (try 'Goldstar' and 'Macabee') are available on draught; imported European beers are of better quality but very expensive. Make sure you sample (but not perhaps in the pub!) Israeli malt beer, which is sweet, refreshing and non-alcoholic ('Nesher' is the most famous brand).

Drinking alcohol (beer) in the street is bad form. In the summer you will find that many people carry bottled water and sip this incessantly. It is very easy to become dehydrated in the Israeli summer: drink much more water than you would normally, even if you are not thirsty. Tap water is perfectly safe to drink but has a less-than-pleasant taste. There are many competing brands of bottled spring water which you should try.

Public drunkenness is rare and is considered very inappropriate behaviour. You will find the occasional drunken youth. Most drunks are, regrettably, foreign visitors.

3

Home Visits

'Easy-going family atmosphere'

The family is still an exceedingly significant institution in Israeli culture and the home is the celebration of the family. The average family tends to be hospitable and easy-going. You will probably be invited into a number of homes during your visit and you should look forward to these occasions. You should expect to meet the wife and the children, as well as any other relative or neighbour who happens to have drifted in.

Invited guests usually arrive late – say, 15 to 30 minutes – and this is not considered impolite. However, if a longer delay is anticipated – telephone your host. Not to show up for an invitation is considered exceedingly rude, unless there is an exceptional excuse.

The traditional custom is for the host to greet his visitor with *baruch ha'ba* – 'blessed is the one who comes'. You might also hear the plural form 'b'ruchim ha'bayim'. Traditionally, the visitor responds *baruch ha'nimtza* – 'blessed is the one who is found here' (the plural form is *b'ruchim ha'nimtzayim*) – but increasingly this is regarded as a bit formal.

Guests usually bring a gift, such as a bottle of wine, a box of chocolates, a small potted plant etc. Flowers are not usually brought unless you are visiting before a festival (e.g. *shabbat*) or on someone's birthday, anniversary etc. Overly ostentatious gifts may produce feelings of awkwardness and should be avoided.

Since children occupy a very significant place in the Israeli family, consider buying a small gift (toy, book etc) appropriate for the age, and number, of your host's children. Make sure that you do not leave anyone out.

Family atmospheres tend to be easy-going. Expect to meet the children and be prepared to let them practise their English on you. Do not be afraid to coax them, they will initially act shyly or appear to be shy.

You will be expected to relax and your host will be alarmed if you do not do so. Snacks (fruit, nuts, sunflower seeds, popcorn etc) will be offered as will drinks (fruit juice, soda etc). You will be expected to accept and eat at least a token amount. Not to do so will be taken as a sign of undue reserve.

Smoking is much more prevalent in Israel than in many other Western countries. There is, however, increasing public awareness of the dangers of smoking and of smoke-filled environments. Ask for your host's permission if you want to smoke; increasingly, your request will

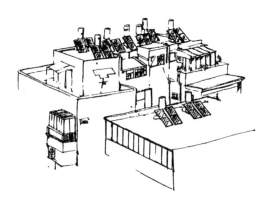

Solar panels on the rooftops

be denied, or you will be taken out onto the balcony (*merpeset*).

Family seating, dynamics and conversations are more likely to reflect the ethnic origin of your hosts. It is not uncommon in many homes for men and women to sit and talk separately. Keep your eyes on your host, or other guest, for possible cues. Israelis enjoy their households and want you to do the same.

If invited to dine, remember to complement whoever prepared the meal. Curiosity about dishes, requests for recipes etc are considered polite, but avoid ornate praise; it will be considered insincere.

Communicate the fact that you are having a pleasurable experience during the visit and as you leave. While not required, consider telephoning the following day to express your thanks; it will be appreciated. Avoid the risk of being seen as a stiff-shirt or snob, incapable of enjoying hospitality or friendship.

Israeli apartments are often very small. A sleep-over guest involves considerable family logistics for your host, but this will be worked out quietly to accommodate you. It is considered polite to recognize this effort. Do not be distracted, however, by the casual approach of your host family. Israeli hospitality only attains its full beauty when it is offered, accepted and acknowledged.

If taking a shower in your host's apartment remember that all hot water comes from a (small) solar collector on the roof. While this provides piping hot water, it is inconsiderate to take an over-long shower. Incidentally, building codes in Israel prohibit electrical switches from being located inside the bathroom. Light switches are obvious but the master switch to the electric wall heater is outside. If you are going to use the heater, make sure that it is on before you enter.

Children of Israel – much-loved and indulged

$$\boxed{4}$$

Out & About

THE PUBLIC TRANSPORT SYSTEM

The public bus system within, and between, cities is excellent. The second largest bus company in the world is 'Egged', outranked only by London's public transport system.

The city fare is standard no matter how many stops you travel through. Incidentally, when talking about buses Israelis – as in many European languages – use the word 'stations' (*tachanot*) in the same way as the English use 'stops'. As in other countries, bus-drivers are often under a great deal of pressure and might be far from sociable. If approached in a friendly manner you will probably find that most bus-drivers do speak English, and do know the best way for you to get to your destination: make use of them.

Within the city, queuing etiquette at bus-stops is very informal. Being first in line does not necessarily mean that you can expect to board first. On the bus it is considered proper to give up one's seat for an obviously older man or woman, or for a noticeably pregnant woman. Children still tend to give up their seats to their elders, but do not count on it.

Inter-city buses are usually air-conditioned. At central bus stations tickets should be bought from the ticket kiosk (*kupah*) before queuing for the bus. Formal queuing etiquette is in force here. Expect mild pushing, but refrain from this yourself.

Never leave luggage unattended in a public place. Israelis, regrettably with very good cause, are very security conscious. Suspicious objects will be instantly reported to the police and you will return to find a crowd of spectators watching – from a safe distance – your packages being detonated by a police bomb-disposal team. If the police trace the neglected items back to their owner, he/she will be summarily fined.

As a matter of civic responsibility Israeli bus passengers will often ask for owners of items (e.g. the case which you placed on that unoccupied bus seat) to identify themselves. Do not view this as undue interference in your business.

You may find inter-city shared taxis (*sherut*) faster. These operate between all of the major cities and have a fixed route and fare. A similar service (for example 'Nesher Taxis') is available 24-hours a day for those going to Ben Gurion International Airport.

The *sherut* will either be a seven-seater Mercedes or minibus and will be air-conditioned. The driver will wait until all of the places in his vehicle are filled. If the passengers are in a hurry, and if one or two places remain unfilled, they may agree to share the cost of the remaining places among themselves. It is always advisable to settle on the exact fare before the journey begins. The *sherut* driver is never tipped.

TAXIS AND CARS

Taxi fares are determined according to an official tariff and drivers are required by law to turn on their meters, unless a specific fare has been mutually agreed upon. Taxi-drivers must provide you with a receipt (a print-out from their meter) which includes details of their business identification.

Drivers often quote a fare for the journey instead of turning on their meter. You should not agree to this unless you are familiar with the journey and with the average meter fare. If in any doubt – or if you simply prefer – insist that the driver turn on his meter. If he refuses take another taxi.

Official fares are posted (in English) on the inside of the taxi. All taxis must be registered and show an identifying number on a roof-mounted sign. At night the sign, and identifying number, are illuminated. This number can be reported to the police if you encounter a serious problem with your taxi-driver.

Taxi-drivers are relatively well paid and would not be tipped by an Israeli. It is quite common for tourists to tip, and some drivers may pressure you to do so, but it is not required.

If you wish to rent your own car you will find that relatively straight forward. In Jerusalem some visitors make a point of renting a car from the eastern (predominantly Arab) part of the city, believing that the prominent Arabic door- and window-stickers will safeguard them against any Palestinian hostilities. A black-and-white head covering (*kafiya*) and copy of the Koran are sometimes supplied for prominent dashboard display. Unless you plan extensive touring into troubled areas this subterfuge is quite unnecessary. Do not expect your Israeli host to sympathize with such a strategy.

Driving is one of the least attractive things about Israel; it tends to bring out a great deal of latent frustration and aggression. While driver education (and reeducation) is extensive it might be hard for you to notice this. Anticipate poor lane discipline, aggression, impatience, spontaneous bouts of horn pounding and general lack of motoring courtesy. You have been warned!

PUBLIC PLACES

Pedestrians are well cared for in Israel. In larger cities streets are closed off to traffic, letting you enjoy window-shopping, street performers, open-air cafes or simply strolling. People appear when the sun has set; you will find the down-town streets of Jerusalem filled at 2 a.m. Street crime is exceedingly low.

Hotel lobbies are very popular places to conduct business meetings. Order coffee if you feel self-conscious, but check the prices first of all.

It is considered socially inept to leave your possessions unattended; security is a sensitive issue. Similarly, avoid any object which does not seem to have an owner.

Policemen and policewomen wear blue uniforms and usually speak English. The paramilitary police (Border Police) are heavily armed, wear a dark green uniform with beret of a similar colour. Border Police are less likely to speak English.

When asked for directions many Israelis dislike displaying their ignorance, especially if they are residents of the city. They will be keen to suggest possible routes, buses to take, etc. It is always best to offer thanks, set out in the indicated direction and then ask someone else when discreet to do so. Do not be annoyed or perplexed if the first person misdirected you; Israelis do not like to admit that they do not know something!

QUEUING

Queuing is less significant in Israel than it once was but it does have its own etiquette. There are two kinds of queue: formal (those requiring a number) and informal (where no number is required). When joining a formal queue (government ministries, health clinics etc) be sure to obtain a number from the ticket dispenser. A display will probably indicate the number being requested and the official (*pakid*) to be seen. Wait your turn patiently. If you are the sort of person who enjoys poking sticks into beehives to see what happens, ignore the number and move up to the head of the line.

In informal queues (banks, airports etc) if you have some other errand to do (in the same building) you can save your place. Imagine Y is behind X. Y says 'I am after you' and leaves. It is good manners for X to advise newcomer Z that Y has a reserved place. When Y returns he/she should advise Z 'I was here' (if necessary X will confirm this). It is polite for Y to thank X. All of this can be done in English – preferably with a smile and a hand gesture.

Because of this system of saving places, you might think that people are simply pushing into the queue in front of you. Be assured that this is not so; only those who have made prior arrangements will be tolerated.

5

Conversation & Communication

Non-military matters

INTRODUCTIONS

The handshake is obligatory on meeting and departing. It should be a firm, deliberate, but not too energetic gesture. A limp handshake might be interpreted as insincere symptomatic of a weak personality.

When shaking a person's hand look directly into his/her eyes. Never remain seated when shaking a standing person's hand. Always make an effort to rise; the more you rise the greater equality of status you show. In Israel it is potentially dangerous to make assumptions about your assumed status, or to assume that others are unaware of the presumptions you harbour!

Yes, people do say *shalom* (literally 'peace') when being introduced, or when meeting one another – just as you may have seen in films or read in books. The correct response is *shalom u'vracha* (peace and blessing)) but you will more often hear *na'eem m'od* (a pleasure), especially if you are being introduced for the first time.

When seeing an old friend whom you have not seen for some time the more formal (and archaic) greeting is *shalom alechem* (literally 'peace be with you'). The appropriate response is *alechem shalom*. Such a greeting is very formal and a bit old-fashioned.

Young people often use the English (that is to say the American) 'Hi', or the Arabic *'Ahalan*, when they meet. They may also use the colloquial *ma'nisha* (how are you), or *ma' ha'inyanin* (what's going on) but these would probably sound inappropriate coming from a non-Israeli.

When you telephone, people will either answer with *shalom* or – increasingly common – 'alo', which you undoubtedly realize is the local form of 'hello'.

Among men, putting a hand on a shoulder or back-slapping is quite common but you should not initiate this. Likewise it is acceptable for long-time friends (men) to hug enthusiasti-cally and to kiss one another on the cheeks when meeting. Unless you do have a long-standing friendship with the person being introduced do not initiate this.

Among the young, same gender physical contact is quite acceptable; teenage girls walk together arm-in-arm, and you will see a lot of hugging among male soldiers. Men and women tend not to touch in public although

'. . .arm in arm'

such expressions of affection would probably not raise too many eyebrows.

During a conversation the speaker's hands might be used more actively than you are accustomed to. Remember that this hand language complements the spoken word; focus on the lips and eyes, not the hands. Feel free to use your own hands to stress a point, but do not overdo this; it would be considered inappropriate mimicry.

Israelis will use first names when speaking to teachers, army officers and almost anybody else; it is a sign of friendliness. After you have been introduced people will either address you by your first name, or ask if they can do so. If they do not, invite them to call you by your first name.

Be aware that when being introduced some Israelis give their family name first. This is particularly likely to happen on the telephone or in written correspondence. If in doubt as to which name is which, it would be expected that you ask for clarification.

Academics often expect you to use 'Doctor' or 'Professor' plus their family name. Israeli academics are particularly jealous of prestige; do not play lightly with their academic ranks.

Most Israeli men you meet have a dual life: a civilian and a military one. They also tend to keep these lives in separate compartments. Retired military officers – or currently active officers on reserve duty – should not be referred to by their rank. You may see former rank (or reserve duty rank) mentioned in a résumé, but this is simply to indicate accomplishment – and to activate the Israeli version of the old boys' network.

When leaving somebody you can say *shalom*, or *shalom, shalom*, or *l'hitra'ot* (the Hebrew equivalent of the French *'au revoir'*). In a very casual setting – particularly if the speaker is in a rush to leave – 'bye' (the contraction of 'goodbye') is commonly used.

CONVERSATION

When talking, Israeli males may stand closer to you than you are used to. If you feel claustrophobic it is alright to back up; the one speaking to you will probably think you are one of those cold-blooded northerners.

During a conversation a hand may be momentarily placed on your arm. This contact is meant to communicate concern; to show interest in you as a human being; to emphasize a point, or simply to reassure you. It is best not to initiate physical contact, especially if you are known to be a northerner (American, British etc).

It is normal for an Israeli to look directly into someone's face when speaking to them. To look indirectly at them, or to fix one's gaze on the distance between you, might signify disinterest, disagreement or worse.

As with all Mediterranean countries, you will find that hands are often used to dramatize the conversation. You will be able to get much more insight into what the speaker intends, however, by watching his/her lips and eyes, rather than hands.

There is a very prevalent hand-sign for 'Just a moment, please'. With the palm upwards, the tips of all the fingers are brought together. The hand is then moved back and forward several times. This is usually accompanied by a facial expression indicating annoyance, reservation or entreatment – depending on the situation. The general rule when outside your own culture is to avoid all hand gestures: they can lead to considerable confusion or embarrassment.

When indicating that something is incorrect, many Israelis make a slight 'tut' with the tongue on the back of the upper front teeth. This is not a sign of annoyance or disapproval.

LANGUAGE

Most Israelis have studied English at school and many speak it very well. You will be able to use English in almost every situation. Israelis are often keen to practise their language skills on you. American usage of English predominates, including slang and spelling. You will not be expected to speak Hebrew, but obviously a few words and phrases could be useful. Some of these have been included near the end of this book.

Opinions differ as to whether a very basic set of foreign-language skills impresses your hosts, or simply accentuates your ignorance of their culture. This is certainly an issue in

Israel where Hebrew is quite difficult to learn and a high level of English is spoken. Indeed, you will often see Israelis, unable to comprehend someone's poor Hebrew, demanding he/she speak in English – or French, or Spanish, or Yiddish. (Yiddish, the German-based *lingua franca* of European Jews, is spoken by many older Israelis.)

Do not be deterred. Hebrew is a second language for about 60% of Israelis. Sprinkle a few basic Hebrew words into your conversation. This will be recognized as a positive gesture. Remember that while English is widely spoken and understood, it is probably the second, third or even fourth language of your listener. If what you are saying is crucial make sure that he/she has fully understood you.

Generally, an Israeli will have no hesitation in stopping you if what was said was unclear. Still, it is your responsibility – as user of the active language – to ensure that crucial matters are understood properly by your listener.

You will probably want to read the country's oldest English-language daily newspaper, The *Jerusalem Post*, for a good mix of local and international news. Should you want to hear the news in English, you can do so by listening to the radio – *Kol Yisrael* (Voice of Israel). Tune to AM 576 (KHz) or 1458. While the English language section of *Kol Yisrael* seems to be constantly shrinking, you can hear English news programmes from 07:00 to 07:15; 13:00 to 13:05, and 18:00 to 18:30. You can also listen to the BBC World Service on AM 639 or 1323 throughout most of the day.

Israelis are avid news listeners: the radio is inevitably turned on in the bus or taxi. A knowledge of the day's domestic news stories will not only help you to a better understanding of this small country, it will indicate your empathy with its people – the mark of a trusted friend.

EMOTIONS AND FEELINGS

Israelis often display very emotional behaviour in public. It is perhaps best to think of Israel as a gigantic, extended family where the emotions of the family – tenderness, concern, anger, frustration – help bind members more closely together. Family emotions, of course, are best restricted to the home and should not be displayed on the street. Personal bickering, or personal concerns, will evaporate in a moment if a major family (national) crisis develops.

This sense of inclusion and concern is perhaps one of the most wonderful aspects of living in Israel, but remember that Israelis delineate strictly between those who are inside – or outside – their extended national family. As a visitor Israelis will, as it were, present you with

the family album and suppress the really interesting inner emotions which make the family so interesting.

Angry outbursts – often the result of frustration – occur quite frequently between Israelis. It is considered rude to subject a visitor to this kind of outburst, and even for a visitor to have to witness one of these 'domestic' scenes. This may be different to the way people conduct themselves in your own country, but remember that this volatility is part of the normal way of Israeli life.

In spite of often intense exchanges, the parties involved quickly calm down, rarely hold grudges and try to part on fairly civil terms – even though an apology is rarely expected, or offered.

TABOOS

Israelis seem to have an opinion on everything, which they will be pleased to share with you, regardless of your inclination or their expertise. Given this forwardness, are there any subjects which are taboo in conversation?

In the Tonga language taboo has a range of meanings, extending from 'holy' to 'private'. In Israel, few topics should be considered banned, but there are a number which have a degree of 'holiness/privateness' and should be avoided.

These topics, listed below, are, of course, very widely discussed by Israelis who can become wildly passionate about them. It would be considered presumptuous of you, however, to discuss them. It would be thought that you lacked either the knowledge or moral rectitude – and you would be told as much.

- The Holocaust.
- The treatment of Palestinian detainees.
- Military applications of nuclear energy.
- Religion.
- Anti-semitic jokes.

The last item might seem surprisingly obvious but remember that much Jewish humour is self-critical – even self-deprecating – and while this may bring a smile when told by a Jew to Jews the same joke would be seen as offensive when told by a non-Jew. Do not be inadvertently lulled into a sense of being 'inside' the culture.

Hand-sign for 'Just a moment, please'

6

Religion

The kippa

How could we talk about Israel without talking about religion? You may be have experience of religion as a state institution, or as a separate, spent force in the predominantly secular world of the 1990s. However, in Israel, religious identity is more tenacious and more contentious. It is an involved and emotive area for Israelis: be careful.

The State of Israel is a secular, but fundamentally Jewish, state. Pluralism is professed – with all religions welcome to practise their faiths and given free access to their holy places – but it would be naïve to consider the State of Israel as anything other than a profoundly Jewish expression of aspiration and national identity. There is no state religion but most areas of domestic law (personal status, marriage, divorce, funerals etc) are controlled by the Rabbinate. The Rabbinate also ensure that Jewish dietary laws are observed in most (but not all) public places, including tourist hotels.

There is a wide spectrum of Jewish, religious observance in Israel. There is no neat polarization, although there are certainly extreme groupings at either side of the spectrum. Low religious observance does not mean antipathy towards Judaic values and tradition. For instance:

- 67% of all Jews fast on Yom Kippur (the Day of Atonement).
- 50% keep separate sets of utensils for eating milk or meat.
- only 20% of the population identifies as totally non-observant.
- 14% identifies as totally observant.

Judaism is not a narrowly defined religion: it is a broad system of beliefs and cultural values which permeates much of the life of even the secular Israeli. What you will most likely notice are the ultra-Orthodox: men with side-locks, dressed in black hats and long coats, the women in long skirts, dark stockings and covered heads (silk scarves or, confusingly, very natural-looking wigs).

They tend to live life separate from the rest of Israel; indeed, some are very antagonistic to the very concept of a Jewish State. The men may well spend all of their time studying Jewish Law although some are shopkeepers or independent businessmen. As a group they tend to keep to themselves and probably feel that they have little in common with you. If you enter ultra-Orthodox areas dress modestly (women should wear skirts), behave with decorum and do not photograph the inhabitants.

Segmentation of the Jewish world is always problematic, however you will also probably notice Traditional Jews. They represent a wide spectrum of Orthodox observance. Men wear a *kippa* (skullcap) – often crocheted – and the basic rule is that the larger, and blacker the *kippa* the further the wearer is to the religious right.

When dealing with religious Israelis here are a few points to keep in mind:

- In religious circles male-female contact is discouraged. You may find a handshake declined. The declining person realizes that you are unaware of the custom; do not feel in any way rejected. Smile, bow your head slightly and sheepishly withdraw the offending hand.

- Avoid sitting beside a religious person of the other gender. If you look carefully you will see that religious men and women sit separately on the bus (except if they are husband and wife).

- *Shabbat* (the sabbath) begins before sunset on Friday, and ends after sunset on Saturday. In observant circles all weekday work (cooking, working, buying, travelling etc) is suspended. Government offices, banks and most businesses are closed from midday Friday. Increasingly, government and business are moving to a five-day week, with Friday and *shabbat* official holidays. You will note that in Jerusalem (where 35% of the population identify as religious) all public transport stops.

- Jewish festivals are set according to the lunar calendar, which means that their dates move with respect to civil calendar years. Since festivals have similar restrictions as *shabbat*, check with a Jewish calendar when scheduling meetings and excursions.

- It is rare for an Israeli Jew to have close contact with Christians. This – and an exceedingly long history of Christian persecution, forced conversion, and missionary activity – make Christian-Jewish debate sensitive. Visiting Christians are warmly welcomed in Israel and free to practise their faith but a heightened degree of religious awareness is a must.

- When visiting a Jewish holy place the rule is to limit the amount of exposed flesh. Men should have their heads covered and preferably not wear shorts. Women need not cover their heads (although many do) but should preferably wear a skirt or dress. They may find that a light scarf, or shawl, draped over the shoulder fulfills the requirement of both comfort and modesty.

Ultra-Orthodox Jews in festive clothes.
[Older man's fur hat is a *shtriemal*]

- Because of the intricacies of customs and Jewish law it is not common for a non-Jew to be invited to a religious home on *shabbat* or a festival. Should you receive such an invitation you will obviously not be expected to know what constitutes correct behaviour. If your host has inadvertently failed to explain what can, or cannot, be done you should raise the issue directly with him/her.

Ultra-Orthodox Jewish women saying Psalms at the Wailing Wall

7

Business Matters

'Things are often hectic in Israel'

'JUGGLING' FOR TIME

While punctuality is not an Israeli virtue, try to be on time for business appointments; it is expected of non-Israelis.

Israel has what cross-cultural scholars call a 'polychronic' culture, where it is common to do a number of different things at the same time. Israelis must juggle with many competing demands – business, family, bureaucracies, reserve duty in the army, ever volatile political environments – and be able to put a social gloss on the whole assortment. Under this bombardment of time-demands Israelis consider a polychronic approach natural. Americans, by contrast, are 'monochronic' and are often considered to be unduly preoccupied with time and scheduling.

Occasionally, the person with whom you are meeting will delay an appearance for some time believing that it conveys higher status; this obviously is a strategy which can backfire if punctuality or timeliness are part of the way you do business.

It might help to keep the following in mind:

- Things are often hectic in Israel and delays can occur.
- If you are kept waiting do not feel manipulated or slighted.
- If you consider time a serious issue consider explaining your own cultural attitudes towards it in a positive, firm manner.

THE ENVIRONMENT OF BUSINESS

Remember that the Israeli economy lurched – or more accurately is still in the process of lurching – from monolithic, state-controlled monopolies to private-sector markets. This means that a new way of doing business is having to be learned: altered management styles, production schedules, marketing approaches, customer satisfaction, increased product reliability and quality. Israeli business people are very fast learners, but make sure that the admirable person you are dealing with has suppliers and sub-contractors who share his (or her) understanding of the altered business environment.

Remember that Israelis generally want to please in business situations. They often promise what they might not be able to deliver. A culture of customer satisfaction – timeliness in meeting schedules, customer responsiveness, professional business ethics, reliability – is still in the formative stage. There is a great amount of goodwill but make sure that it does not obscure the practical realities.

So far as managerial decision-making is concerned, remember that Israelis have what the textbooks call 'a low power distance'. This means that managers prefer to be consulted by their seniors when decisions involving them are being made. An authoritarian, directive management style is resented. Be aware that consultative preference often results in what you might consider a directionless overflow of opinions, suggestions and reservations. Resist trying to impose premature order; an agreement will eventually emerge.

Keep in mind that Israelis have what researchers call 'a low-context culture'. In high-context cultures listeners will respond to the status of the speaker – and the setting – as much as to the actual content of the speech. Thus, an older representative of the firm will command attention because of his age. This is not the case in Israel. Israelis will be more interested in content rather than context, so:-

- Keep your business presentation short and crisp.
- Avoid elaborate prose or excessive rhetoric.
- Be prepared to face questions and debate.
- Do not simply repeat a point, or raise your voice.
- Be prepared to listen to dissent.

Regarding women and the workplace, try to keep in mind the following somewhat paradoxical facts:-

- Women, unless exempted (usually for religious reasons) serve two years in the Israeli Defence Forces. They serve in more than 500 of the 800 military job classifications but are under-represented at all senior ranks.

- Women enjoy the same legal and social rights as men.

- Women are prominent in lower level managerial positions but often a 'glass ceiling' exists to restrict their further advancement.

- With notable exceptions, the male Israeli's attitude to women is in the 'mildly chauvinistic' to 'acutely macho' range.

None of the above should deter a visiting businesswoman from succeeding in Israel. She will be treated well and will be able to do serious business with her Israeli counterpart. However, in spite of what you may have heard to the contrary, this is not a country where men and women are on a truly equal footing.

GIFTS IN BUSINESS

Gift-giving in business settings can be awkward; you want to convey the pleasure while not appearing to influence. Larger organizations (particularly those owned by the State) prohibit employees from accepting gifts, or limit the amount which they can receive. Bribery is not unknown in Israel but it is punished severely.

If you know the person (from previous contacts), consider bringing a small gift to be given in a personal capacity. Often, people will let you know about items which they are trying to get; these can be given as a gift when you arrive, despite the protests of the recipient. Again, remember that excessive generosity or ostentatious gift-giving is often suspect.

If in doubt, a good whisky – either a blended one such as 'Chivas Regal', or a fine single malt – is considered a substantial and acceptable gift. Unlike other forms of alcohol, whisky is expensive in Israel and has no local imitators. If possible, buy in a duty-free store in transit. Check your calendar: do not give a bottle of whisky immediately before, or during, Passover!

Neckties, pins for neckties and cufflinks are not going to be worn in Israel, whereas a lapel pin with company logo might be.

OTHER THINGS TO KEEP IN MIND

Dress is usually very informal and does not convey status. You should dress well. While it is rare to see an Israeli wearing a necktie do not feel inhibited about wearing one if you want to. There is no formality about exchanging business cards as, say, in Japan. Your English-language card will present no problems.

Communication with the people back home is no problem for the business person. Good international telephone connections and

'. . .rare to see an Israeli wearing a necktie'

faxes abound. Many Israelis seem permanently bound to their beepers and cellular telephones (*Pelaphones* – literally 'wonder 'phones'). Summoned by these devices people will scuttle off to the corners of the room and engage in secretive conversations. If your ears are sharp, and your Hebrew good, you might discover that the conversation is about the menu for supper or what shopping he should do on the way back from the office. The content was not significant; the flirtation with new technology was!

Business will undoubtedly be conducted in English but if for any reason a translator is employed:-

- Articulate clearly and do not rush your presentation.

- When the translation is being made look at your audience for feedback in the form of facial expression, body language etc.

- Rather than simply repeat, restate in a different form.

It is not uncommon for men to carry handguns, usually tucked discreetly into waist bands and covered with the shirt. This should cause you neither alarm nor trepidation. Remember that almost all adult males in Israel have served in the army; that Israeli males are often concerned with a 'macho' image, and that Israel does have very real security difficulties. It would be thought indiscreet (or inept) to make reference to the gun – unless you are an expert in such matters, when an extended conversation on the relative merits of the weapon is possible.

Finally, you should be aware of the thing which every Israeli tries to avoid being: the *frier* (Yiddish: 'a free person'). You will not find this word in your standard phrase book, but it is one which you must understand.

The Israeli's response to alienating and bureaucratic cultures is to develop a network of influential friends and associates capable of cutting through red tape. One measure of an Israeli's power is the extent of this informal network, referred to by the Russian word *Protektzia* (resident Americans sometimes call this 'Vitamin P').

By doing favours, Israelis usually recognize that an obligation has been created; in a very crude sense, nobody does something for nothing. The balancing of favour and obligation is subtle, with no formal score-card being completed. Obligations can be cancelled by the one who granted the favour, and frequently are.

A *frier* is someone who has no *Protektzia*. He is 'free' in the sense of having no value, or worth. An Israeli will gladly do you a favour, so long as you recognize that it *is* a favour. If you presume to treat him as a cypher, devoid of personal discretion and/or social influence, then you treat him as a *frier*. Be cautioned: the *frier* may strike back unexpectedly simply to show that he does have power – in spite of what might have been assumed.

Tiberius: new & old architecture

8

Useful Phrases & Vocabulary

פלאפל זמיר
מיוחד

נקי וטעים
לחיילים הגנחה

A typical 'take-away' meal: *pita* bread *falafel* comprising various sauces and salads

Hebrew is not an exceptionally difficult language to learn. Every year thousands of new immigrants learn basic spoken Hebrew in interactive language classes (*ulpan*). Twenty years ago all immigrants were expected to speak their new language and worked hard to do that. For someone – including a tourist – to ask a question in any other language would have resulted in a stony stare.

Things are different today. A massive increase of new immigrants from the former USSR; an increase in tourism, and a slow reduction of national prickliness mean that you can hear – or speak – almost any language in the street. In spite of what Israelis would have you believe most of them speak good to excellent English. If you insist on using English you will often find that you get better service: tourists are afforded better treatment than locals.

Do learn a little Hebrew and do not be afraid to use it. It will demonstrate your interest in the country. The Hebrew language has united the Jewish people in prayer and in scholarship for many thousands of years. Its revival as a modern spoken language (mainly through the efforts of Eliezer Ben-Yehuda, 1858–1922) is seen as symbolic of the restored national identity of Israel.

USEFUL WORDS AND PHRASES

Pronunciation

a	–	as in fear
ai	–	as in fair
e	–	as in pen
ee	–	as in feet
ie	–	as in lie
o	–	as in on
oe	–	as in bone
u	–	as in put

Consonants as in English except: ch – as in the Scottish 'loch' or the German 'ich'.

In modern Hebrew the stress usually falls on the final syllable. In Hebrew, verbs and nouns agree with the gender (male/female) of the subject. The feminine form is shown in parentheses.

Mr . . .	A-don . . .
Mrs/Ms . . .	Ge-veh-ret . . .

Good morning	*Boe-ker tov*
Good evening	*Eh-rev tov*
Good night (on retiring)	*Lie-la tov*
Goodbye	*L'-heet-ra-ot*
Yes	*Ken*
No	*Lo*
(That's) correct	*Na-chon*
O.K. (It's fine)	*B'-seh-der*
Thank you	*Toe-da*
No, thank you	*Lo, toe-da*
Please (You're welcome)	*B'va-ka-sha*
Excuse me	*S'-lach lee*
My name is . . .	*Sh'mee . . .*
Where is the . . .	*Ai-foe*
I would like . . .	*A-nee ro-tze (ro-tza)*
I'm looking for . . .	*A-nee me-cha-pes (me-cha-pes-et)*
How much does it cost?	*Ka-ma o-leh?*
I don't speak Hebrew	*A-nee lo me-da-ber (me-da-ber-et) Eev-reet*
I don't understand	*A-nee lo mai-veen (me-vee-na)*
Do you understand me?	*Mai-veen (me-vee-na) oe-tee?*
Do you speak English?	*Me-da-ber (me-da-ber-et) Angleet?*
To the right	*Ya-mee-na*
To the left	*S'-mo-la*
Straight ahead	*Ka-dee-ma*
Here	*Kan*
There	*Sham*
Where do you live?	*Ai-fo a-ta gar (at ga-ra)?*
Stop! (for something in motion)	*A-tzor*

VOCABULARY REFERRED TO IN THIS BOOK

'Ahalan — (Arabic)

Alechem shalom — literally: unto you peace. The correct response to *shalom alechem*

baruch ha'ba (plural: *b'ruchim ha'bayim*) — blessed is the one who comes. (Greeting when welcoming visitors.)

b'ruchim ha'bayim l'Eretz Yisrael! — Welcome to Israel!

baruch ha'nimtza (plural: *b'ruchim ha'nimtzayim*) — blessed is the one who is found here. (The traditional response of a received visitor.)

b'tai'avon — Hebrew version of *bon appétit*.

chatzelim — egg plant or aubergine.

chutz l'aretz — literally: outside the Land of Israel. Very often contracted to *chu'l*.

falafel — balls of chickpea batter, fried and served with salads and condiments in pita bread.

frier — (Yiddish). Someone who lacks social clout or influence.

garanim — literally: seeds. Roasted sunflower or watermelon seeds.

kafiya — (Arabic). Flowing head-cover worn by male Arabs.

kashrut — literally: fitness. Pertaining to things which are suitable for religious use, particularly food.

kibbutz (plural: *kibbutzim*) — collective farms.

kippa — a skullcap worn by religious men.

Kol Yisrael	– The Voice of Israel – an Israeli radio corporation.
kupah	– literally: a box. Where you buy your bus tickets.
l'hitra'ot	– Hebrew for *au revoir*.
l'hitra'ot ba'aretz	– see you back in Israel.
l'vri'ut	– to your health. Used in the same way as *bon appétit*.
l'chaim	– to life. The traditional toast among Jews.
ma ha'inyanim	– literally: what's of interest? Colloquial form of greeting.
ma'nishma	– how are you?
merpeset	– a balcony. Most Israeli houses have one or more.
na'eem m'od	– it's a great pleasure (. . . to have met you).
pakid	– a clerk/official.
Pelaphones	– literally: wonder phones. The ubiquitous cellular telephone.
Protektzia	– (Russian). Influence to change/expedite bureaucratic/political decisions.
sabra	– the fruit of the prickly pear cactus which you can buy in the summer from street vendors. Colloquially: a native-born Israeli.
S/fardim	– literally: Spaniards. Descendants of Jews expelled from Spain in 1492 and who developed communities along the Mediterranean.
shabbat	– the Sabbath (It's the same word). The seventh day of rest, which in Israel is Saturday.

shalom	– peace. Commonly used as a greeting.
shalom alechem	– peace be with you. (An archaic form of greeting used in formal – especially religious – settings.)
shalom u'vracha	– peace and blessing. The formal response given when someone says *shalom*.
sherut	– literally: a service. Inter-city taxis where all of the passengers share the fare.
sh'warma	– (Arabic). Slices of freshly roasted meat served in a large pita roll.
tachana (plural: *tachanot*)	– literally: a station. A bus-stop. the central bus station is *tachana merkazit*.
ulpan	– Intensive programme for learning Hebrew.

Mobile cart selling bagels – a Jewish staple food

9

Did You Know?

Jaffa (Tel Aviv) – the oldest working port in the world

The Israeli unit of currency is the New Israeli Shekel (abbreviated to NIS). Banknotes exist for 200, 100, 50, 20 and 10 NIS. The 10 NIS note is currently being replaced by a coin of that value. There are also 5 and 1 NIS coins. The New Shekel is divided into 100 agurot.

The words 'New Sheqalim' appear (in English) on the reverse of all banknotes. Look for this until you become familiar with the money. There have been cases of unscrupulous money-changers giving tourists old Israeli banknotes (marked only 'Sheqalim'), which are worthless. Avoid unofficial money-changers!

In an emergency dial 100 for police; 101 for first-aid/ambulance. Do not panic. Speak slowly, in English.

The electricity supply in Israel is 220 volts AC, 50 cycles. Supply is very dependable.

Israel has a land surface of approximately 7,800 square miles. Almost half of this – from Be'er Sheva south to Eilat – is very sparsely populated indeed, while the northern half is fast becoming one of the world's most densely populated regions.

Israelis currently rank as Europe's most avid gamblers. You will see little kiosks on most streets selling tickets for lotteries, sports results competitions, etc. Symptomatic?

Christmas is not celebrated in Israel (except in Christian areas like Bethlehem) but some secular Israelis celebrate 31 December (the civil New Year) which is called 'Silvester'. If sending out end-of-year promotional items to Israeli clients 'Seasons Greetings' is the most diplomatic salutation.

Twenty-five years ago, Israel ranked as one of the most egalitarian industrial states. Today it is ranked second from the bottom (the United States of America is bottom of the list). It shares with America the bottom place for having the highest percentage of its children living below the poverty line: an inevitable consequence of the move towards a market economy.